Nursery Rhymes Poetry Book for kids

Perfect Interactive and Educational Gift for Baby, Toddler 1-3 and 2-4 Year Old Girl and Boy

Mark Steven

NURSERY RHYMES POETRY Books

27 Nursery Rhymes Included:

- Little Miss Muffet
- Old Mother Hubbard
- Jack & Jill
- Itsy Bitsy Spider
- Humpty Dumpty
- It's Raining It's Pouring
- One Two Buckle My Shoe
- Little Bo Peep
- Mary Had a Little Lamb
- Hickory, Dickory, Dock
- Twinkle, Twinkle, Little Star
- Georgie Porgie
- Little Boy Blue

- Baa Baa Black Sheep
- Mary Mary Quite Contrary
- Rain Rain Go Away

- Hey Diddle Diddle
- Little Jack Horner
- Peter Peter Pumpkin Eater
- Rub a Dub Dub
- This Little Piggy
- Jack Be Nimble
- Row Row Row Your Boat
- Rock-a-Bye Baby
- Five Speckled Frogs
- One, Two, Three, Four, Five
- London Bridge

's
____
Nursery
Rhymes
Poetry
Book

Directions: Write the word "a" on each line to complete the poem.

Little Miss Muffet

Little Miss Muffet

Sat on _ tuffet,

Eating her curds and whey;

Along came _ spider,

Who sat down beside her

And frightened

Miss Muffet away!

Name: ___________________________________

Word - the

Directions: Write the word "the" on each line to complete the poem.

Old Mother Hubbard

Old Mother Hubbard

Went to _____ cupboard,

To give _____ poor dog a bone;

When she came there

_____ cupboard was bare,

And so _____ poor

dog had none!

Directions: Write the word "and" on each line to complete the poem.

Jack and Jill

Jack _____ Jill

Went up the hill

To fetch a pail of water.

Jack fell down

_____ broke his crown,

_____ Jill

came tumbling after!

Directions: Write the word "up" on each line to complete the poem.

Itsy Bitsy Spider

The itsy bitsy spider

Climbed ___ the water spout.

Down came the rain

And washed the spider out.

Out came the sun

And dried ___ all the rain

And the itsy bitsy spider

Climbed ___ the spout again!

Directions: Write the word "all" on each line to create
new words and complete the poem.

Humpty Dumpty

Humpty Dumpty sat on a w______,

Humpty Dumpty

had a great f______.

______ the King's horses

And ______ the King's men

Couldn't put Humpty

Together again!

Directions: Write the word "he" on each line to complete the poem.

It's Raining, It's Pouring

It's raining;

It's pouring.

The old man is snoring.

___ went to bed

And bumped his head,

And ___ wouldn't get up

In the morning!

Directions: Highlight the number words with a yellow crayon.

<u>One, Two, Buckle My Shoe</u>

One, two, buckle my shoe.

Three, four, shut the door.

Five, six, pick up sticks.

Seven, eight, lay them straight.

Nine, Ten, a big fat hen.

<u>One, Two, Three, Four, Five</u>

One, two, three, four, five,

Once I caught a fish alive,

Six, seven, eight, nine, ten,

Then I let it go again.

Why did you let it go?

Because it bit my finger so.

Which finger did it bite?

This little finger on the right!

Directions: Write the word "them" on each line to complete the poem.

<u>Little Bo Peep</u>

Little Bo Peep

Has lost her sheep,

and doesn't know where

to find ______;

Leave ______ alone

And they'll come home,

Wagging their tails

Behind ______!

Directions: Write the word "was" on each line to complete the poem.

Mary Had a Little Lamb

Mary had a little lamb,
 Its fleece _____ white as snow,
And everywhere that Mary went,
 The lamb _____ sure to go;
 He followed her
 to school one day-
That _____ against the rule,
It made the children
 laugh and play
 To see a lamb at school.

Name: _______________________________

Directions: Write the word "the" on each line to complete the poem.

Hickory Dickory Dock

Hickory, dickory, dock

_____ mouse ran up

_____ clock.

_____ clock struck one,

_____ mouse ran down.

Hickory, dickory, dock.

Directions: Write the word "for" on each line to complete the poem.

Baa Baa Black Sheep

Baa, baa, black sheep,

Have you any wool?

Yes, sir, yes, sir,

Three bags full;

One _____ the master,

And one _____ the dame,

And one _____ the little boy,

Who lives down the lane.

Directions: Write the word "with" on the line to complete the poem.

Mary, Mary Quite Contrary

Mary, Mary,

Quite contrary,

How does your garden grow?

__________ silver bells,

And cockle shells,

And pretty maids

All in a row!

Name: _______________________
Word - day
Directions: Write the word "day" on the line to complete the poem.
Rain, Rain
Rain, rain
Go away.
Come again
Another
______.

Directions: Write the word "little" on each line to complete the poem.

<u>This Little Piggy</u>

This ________ piggy

went to the market,

This ________ piggy stayed home,

This ________ piggy

had roast beef,

This ________ piggy

had none,

This ________ piggy cried

Wee, wee, wee

all the way home!

Directions: Write the word "be" on each line to complete the poem.

Jack Be Nimble

Jack ___ nimble,

Jack ___ quick,

Jack jump

over the

candlestick.

Directions: Write the word "see" on the line to complete the poem.

Hey Diddle Diddle

Hey diddle diddle,

The cat and the fiddle,

The cow jumped

over the moon.

The little dog laughed,

To _____ such sport,

And the dish ran away

With the spoon!

Directions: Write the word "in" on each line to complete the poem.

Little Jack Horner

Little Jack Horner,

Sat ___ the corner,

Eating a Christmas pie

He put ___ his thumb,

And pulled out a plum,

And said,

"What a good boy

am I!"

Directions: Write the word "her" on each line to complete the poem.

Peter, Peter
Pumpkin Eater

Peter, Peter

pumpkin eater,

Had a wife

but couldn't keep ____;

He put ____ in

a pumpkin shell

And there he kept ____

very well.

Directions: Write the word "out" on the line to complete the poem.

Rub-a-Dub-Dub

Rub-a-dub-dub

Three men in a tub,

And who do you think they be?

The butcher, the baker,

the candlestick

maker-

All set ___

to sea!

Directions: Write the word "down" on the line to complete the poem.

Row, Row, Row Your Boat

Row, row,

row your boat,

Gently _______

the stream.

Merrily, merrily,

Merrily, merrily,

Life is but a dream!

Directions: Write the word "when" on each line to complete the poem.

Rock-a-bye Baby

Rock-a-bye baby,

In the tree top,

_______ the wind blows,

The cradle will rock,

_______ the bough

breaks,

The cradle will fall,

And down will come baby,

Cradle and all.

Directions: Write the word "what" on each line to complete the poem.

Twinkle, Twinkle Little Star

Twinkle, twinkle, little star,

How I wonder _______ you are.

Up above the world so high,

Like a diamond in the sky.

Twinkle, twinkle little star

How I wonder _______ you are.

Name: _________________________ | Word - then |

Directions: Write the word "then" on the line to complete the poem.

Five Little Speckled Frogs

Five little speckled frogs

Sat on a great big log,

Eating the most delicious bugs.

One jumped into the pool,

Where it was nice and cool,

________ there were

four speckled frogs.

Directions: Write the word "play" on the line to complete the poem.

Georgie Porgie

Georgie Porgie,

Puddin' and pie,

Kissed the girls

And made them cry,

When the boys

Came out

To __________,

Georgie Porgie

Ran away!

Directions: Write the word "down" on the line to complete the poem.

London Bridge

London Bridge

Is falling _______,

Falling _______,

Falling _______.

London Bridge

Is falling _______,

My fair lady!

Name: _______________________________

Directions: Write the word "will" on each line to complete the poem.

<u>Little Boy Blue</u>

Little boy blue

Come blow your horn,

The sheep's in the meadow,

The cow's in the corn;

Where is that boy

who looks after the sheep?

Under the haystack fast asleep.

_______ you wake him?

Oh no, not I,

For if I do he _______ surely cry!

Little Miss Muffet

Little Miss Muffet

Sat on a tuffet,

Eating her curds and whey;

Along came a spider,

Who sat down beside her

And frightened

Miss Muffet away!

Old Mother Hubbard

Old Mother Hubbard

Went to the cupboard,

To give the poor dog a bone;

When she came there

the cupboard was bare,

And so the poor

dog had none!

Jack and Jill

Jack and Jill

Went up the hill

To fetch a pail of water.

Jack fell down

and broke his crown,

and Jill

came tumbling after!

Itsy Bitsy Spider

The itsy bitsy spider

Climbed up the water spout.

Down came the rain

And washed the spider out.

Out came the sun

And dried up all the rain

And the itsy bitsy spider

Climbed up the spout again!

Humpty Dumpty

Humpty Dumpty sat on a wall,

Humpty Dumpty

had a great fall.

All the King's horses

And all the King's men

Couldn't put Humpty

Together again!

It's Raining, It's Pouring

It's raining;

It's pouring.

The old man is snoring.

He went to bed

And bumped his head,

And he wouldn't get up

In the morning!

One, Two, Buckle My Shoe

One, two, buckle my shoe.

Three, four, shut the door.

Five, six, pick up sticks.

Seven, eight, lay them straight.

Nine, Ten, a big fat hen.

One, Two, Three, Four, Five

One, two, three, four, five,

Once I caught a fish alive,

Six, seven, eight, nine, ten,

Then I let it go again.

Why did you let it go?

Because it bit my finger so.

Which finger did it bite?

This little finger on the right!

<u>Little Bo Peep</u>

Little Bo Peep

Has lost her sheep,

and doesn't know where

to find them;

Leave them alone

And they'll come home,

Wagging their tails

Behind them!

Mary Had a Little Lamb

Mary had a little lamb,
Its fleece was white as snow,
And everywhere that Mary went,
The lamb was sure to go;
He followed her
to school one day-
That was against the rule,
It made the children
laugh and play
To see a lamb at school.

Hickory Dickory Dock

Hickory, dickory, dock

the mouse ran up

the clock.

the clock struck one,

the mouse ran down.

Hickory, dickory, dock.

Baa Baa Black Sheep

Baa, baa, black sheep,

Have you any wool?

Yes, sir, yes, sir,

Three bags full;

One for the master,

And one for the dame,

And one for the little boy,

Who lives down the lane.

Mary, Mary Quite Contrary

Mary, Mary,

Quite contrary,

How does your garden grow?

with silver bells,

And cockle shells,

And pretty maids

All in a row!

Name: _______________________

Word - day

Rain, Rain

Rain, rain
Go away.
Come again
Another
day.

Name: _______________________

This Little Piggy

This little piggy
went to the market,
This little piggy stayed home,
This little piggy
had roast beef,
This little piggy
had none,
This little piggy cried
Wee, wee, wee
all the way home!

Jack Be Nimble

Jack be nimble,
Jack be quick,
Jack jump
over the
candlestick.

Hey Diddle Diddle

Hey diddle diddle,

The cat and the fiddle,

The cow jumped

over the moon.

The little dog laughed,

To see such sport,

And the dish ran away

With the spoon!

Little Jack Horner

Little Jack Horner,

Sat in the corner,

Eating a Christmas pie

He put in his thumb,

And pulled out a plum,

And said,

"What a good boy

am I!"

Name: _______________________________

Peter, Peter Pumpkin Eater

Peter, Peter

pumpkin eater,

Had a wife

but couldn't keep her;

He put her in

a pumpkin shell

And there he kept her

very well.

Rub-a-Dub-Dub

Rub-a-dub-dub

three men in a tub,

And who do you think they be?

The butcher, the baker,

the candlestick

maker-

All set out

to sea!

Row, Row,
Row Your Boat

Row, row,

row your boat,

Gently down

the stream.

Merrily, merrily,

Merrily, merrily,

Life is but a dream!

Rock-a-bye Baby

Rock-a-bye baby,

in the tree top,

When the wind blows,

the cradle will rock,

When the bough

breaks,

The cradle will fall,

and down will come baby,

Cradle and all.

Twinkle, Twinkle Little Star

Twinkle, twinkle, little star,

how I wonder what you are.

Up above the world so high,

like a diamond in the sky.

Twinkle, twinkle little star

how I wonder what you are.

Five Little Speckled Frogs

Five little speckled frogs

Sat on a great big log,

eating the most delicious bugs.

One jumped into the pool,

where it was nice and cool,

then there were

four speckled frogs.

Georgie Porgie

Georgie Porgie, puddin' and pie,

kissed the girls

and made them cry,

When the boys

came out

to play,

Georgie Porgie

ran away!

London Bridge

London Bridge

is falling down,

falling down,

falling down.

London Bridge

is falling down,

my fair lady!

Little Boy Blue

Little boy blue

come blow your horn.

The sheep's in the meadow,

the cow's in the corn.

Where is that boy

who looks after the sheep?

Under the haystack fast asleep.

Will you wake him?

Oh no, not I,

for if I do he will surely cry!